The Peacock Poems

The Wesleyan Poetry Program: Volume 79

The Peacock Poems

Sherley anne

by Shirley Williams

Wesleyan University Press

Middletown, Connecticut

The publisher gratefully acknowledges the support of the publication of
this book by The Andrew W. Mellon Foundation.

Library of Congress Cataloging in Publication Data

Williams, Shirley Anne, 1944–
    The peacock poems.

    (The Wesleyan poetry program: v. 79)
    I. Title.
PS3573.I45546P4   811'.5'4   75–12531
ISBN 0–8195–2079–9
ISBN 0–8195–1079–3 pbk.

Manufactured in the United States of America

First edition

Evangeline Marie Dusuau

March 25, 1943 — December 26, 1974

. . . and I really love
that woman and grieve
for her in the most
secret reaches of
my heart

this book belong to
Vangy. See Mamma
Ne this what she give
me this what some of
it meant

Contents

. . . the lines converge here . . .

The Peacock Poems

. . . every woman is a victim of the feel blues, too . . .

Any Woman's Blues

Blues is Something to Think About
(the last verse of *One-Sided Bed Blues*)

and this the way that shit come down:

My bed one-sided
    from me sleepin alone so mucha the time.
My bed one-sided, now,
    cause I'm alone so mucha the time.
But the fact that it's empty
    show how this man is messin with my mind.

11

The Valley

The Valley, *i. e.*, the San Joaquin Valley of California; also known as the Central Valley. It lies between California's two great mountain ranges, the Coast Range to the west and the Sierra Nevada to the east. On the south, it is bounded by the Tehachapis, a lesser range. Irrigation of the arid southern half of the Valley and the long growing season, which often begins as early as February, has made farming highly profitable. The economy of the region is based on agriculture and related business and industry, food-processing, the manufacture of farm equipment, and the like. Its principal crops include raisins, figs, cotton, barley, and citrus fruits. The Valley is not the most fertile farming area in the world. It is the richest.

I took the job in L. A. that summer; every month I went back to Ashley to see the doctor. He teased me about going into labor in the Grapevine—that stretch of highway which winds from Tejon Pass to the Valley floor. "I know you know that that's the Valley, too."

Interstate 5 climbs steeply from the floor of the San Fernando Valley into the Tehachapi Mountains. The winds up there are treacherous, the curves and grades deceptive, and I'd almost hold my breath until that spot in the Grapevine, just before the highway makes its final curving descent to the Valley. The world seems to be spread out before you: orange and lemon groves, peach and apricot orchards, grape and cotton fields; the land is onions and alfalfa, sweet melons and packing sheds. The oil derricks to the west aren't visible; neither are the turkey farms and feed lots just over almost any horizon, but I know where they are.

I had hated this, hated all the squat Valley towns; had left, returned, left: The memory of the sun on the dirt and grass graves, on the shiny black skins of my family and friends draws me back.

13

Say Hello to John

I swear I ain't done what Richard
told me bout jumpin round and stuff.
And he knew I wouldn't do nothin to make the baby
come, just joke, say I'mo cough

this child up one day.
So in the night when I felt the water tween
my legs, I thought it was pee and I laid
there wonderin if maybe I was in a dream.

Then it come to me that my water broke and I went
in to tell Ru-ise. *You been havin pains?*
she ask. I hear her fumblin for the light.
Naw, I say. Don't think so. The veins

stand out along her temples. *What time
is it?* Goin on toward four o'clock.
Nigga, I told you:
You ain't havin no babies, not

in the middle of the night.
Get yo ass back to bed.
That ain't nothin but pee. And what
I know bout havin kids cept what she said?

Second time it happen, even she
got to admit this mo'n pee.
And the pain when it come, wa'n't bad
least no mo'n I eva expect to see

again. I remember the doctor smilin,
sayin, Shel, you got a son.
His bright black face above me
sayin, Say hello to John.

If he let us go now

                                    let me strap
the baby in the seat, just don't say
nothin all that while . . .
                                I move round to
the driver side of the car. The air
warm and dry here. Lawd know what it be
in L. A. He open the door for me
and I slide behind the wheel. Baby
facin me lookin without even
blinkin his eye. I wonder if he
know I'm his mamma that I love him
that that his daddy by the door (and
he won't let us go; he still got time
to say wait. Baby blink once but
he only five week old and whatever
he know don't show.
                            His daddy call
my name and I turn to him and wait.
It be cold in the Grapevine at night
this time of year. Wind come whistlin down
through them mountains almost blow this old
VW off the road. I'll be in
touch he say. Say, take care; say, write if
you need somethin.
                            I *will* him to touch
us now, to take care us, to know what
we need is him and his name. He slap
the car door, say, drive careful and turn
to go. If he let us go now . . . how
we gon ever take him back? I ease
out on the clutch, mash in on the gas.
The only answer I get is his back.

A Walk into the Soft Soft

wind through the gathered people
across a land still under
construction: steel girders mute
gesture and silent eye as
anonymous as I the
woman: If anyone had known
to call my name I could not
have owned it.

            Anyone speaks in
fumbling whispers halting words.
Their stifled voices tell of
tenuous contentment a
qualified peace. They all know
my name. It is only I
who cannot say it.

            The wind
ruffles and scatters the dead
dying leaves. They are driven
before that invisible
force in aimless terror. I
hear their dry voice at my door.

Providence

Providence, *n.* 1. The care exercised by God over the universe. 2. An event or circumstance ascribable to divine interposition. 3. The exercise of foresight and care for the future. *Also,* the second largest city in New England, about forty-five miles south-west of Boston. The capital city of Rhode Island, situated in the north-eastern part of the state at the head of Narragansett Bay.

We drove east that summer, just my son and me, catching Interstate 80 at the interchange near the Oakland-Berkeley limits where the highway skirts the Bay. The first day we crossed the northern end of the Valley and the Sierras, covered the desert between Reno and Salt Lake. By sunset, we were into the rolling hilly country on the Utah-Wyoming line, trying to make it to the motel at Little America before it got too late. As we topped each rise, I expected to see the lights of the motel complex on the horizon, but no lights were visible in the gathering dusk.

Interstate 80 plunges and rises, curves, now northward, now south, in that area, always holding stubbornly to an easterly direction. We passed very few cars and on one of those rising curves, I glanced left to where California would be. The sun hadn't quite set; the western sky was a blaze of gold. Then the road curved downward and east again and we continued into the darkness.

17

This Is
a Sad-Ass Poem for a Black Woman to Be Writing

We have not, up to
now, known each other.
The light jive and fly
speech over public
tables do not count
for much.
        I look for
you at your place, in
the few books and bare
walls, even listen
for echoes of you
in the music. I no-
tice an old milk car-
ton; I hear so much
anonymous noise.

You expend yourself —
something — within me
and I pant beneath
you, open, heaving.
You withdraw; I close
and stillness and breath,
bodies burrowing
into damp sheets are
the only sounds in
the silence. Silence:

Good jive, a light rap
and fly speech over
a public table.

2 1/2 Poems: Making Whole

for Leah King

It be cold   cold   cold
    on yo lip   in yo nose
      freeze the tippa yo ear
        wind sweep the sky blue
        and the day be golden

providence

    The campus is an alien thing
        yet even now as I move across it
        the softly voiced calls of How
ya doin   What's hap'nin — Sista
        unsaid and understood — close
        behind me, open before me
        like so many familiar waves in an otherwise
        anonymous sea. Hey now   we call
        Hey now   now   now   now

    Now. But we would not be recognized
        and so hurry away leaving the words
        to hang frosty in the chill Rhode Island
        air.

        Watcha doin way up here — I
        watched the slow almost hidden
        smile   half revealing teeth
        crinkling the cold dyed skin.
        I got a fellowship — she said.
        I can dig it — and I'm grinning but her
        retreating back makes me sad.
        I'd know her in Ca'lina   Texas   Luzan
        but we converge here on the Green
        at Brown in Providence.

    We do not meet.

It be cold   cold   cold
     and the wind, Lawd, the wind
        it sweep that sky blue.

conejo

The field fire send up
     a grey trail to the hazy sky.
     Daddy and Bill speak in smoky
     whispers. "Don't get too close by

     the fire. Watch that baby, Ruise."
     I move way. This side warm
     other side cold. Both
     sides can't get warm

     at once. Ain' no grapes on the vines. I know
     when it be warm, tray grapes turn
     brown, crumple in the sun. They juice
     be sweet and dusty. The sand burn

     yo feet, grit in yo mouth, on yo skin.
     The rows of black vines stretch
     far as I can see. "There one,
     there one," I cry. Bill fetch

     the gun to his shoulder and bam! the gopher
     dead. "How many you make that?"
     "Greens." Daddy spit. "A little
     streak-a-lean, streak-a-fat."

It be cold   cold   cold
     wind sweep the sky blue
        the day be gold.

Time

afternoon

Leslee. Les —
The distance crackles
between us. I dream my child
dead. Born dead.

Honey, it was
a dream. Don't freak because of
that. *Her voice, high and childlike*
made thin through the wires but I
hear what she says   what she means.
. . . *Still. Still —*

Les. *I say it.* Dead
And I got nothin to show
just . . . just my cheeks ridged with rage.

and my cheeks be ridged with rage.

sometime later

I will know what
this all has meant
will have learned what I have learned
I will be older
and this fire will be spent.

sometime

I didn't want to hear what he asked
but he asked it anyway, say, where
my daddy at?

some time, yeah, we have spent in this car
at least half our life together; we

21

had it longer than we ever lived
in any house. It don't matter bout
the places we been, only where we
goin next. Lottsa joy and, well, yeah;
sadness, too, cause even not mindin
bout the places we been, there's always
the leavin . . . The leavin and *next* change
to *been* and to get to *next,* you got
to leave *been.* Yeah, there is sadness and
we been a long time on the road, all
his birthdays, always lookin for the
next with him sittin, then standin right
behind me, right between the bucket
seats, laughin, sleepin, singin, pointin
out the signs along the road.

> The song don't make it past
> my throat. Lawd. Lawd. *Lawd.* I got no
> resources for this day. And the name
> of the place don't mean nothin; he want
> to know why, why he not with me and
> you. I didn't talk about jive niggas
> said nothin about my own rage. What
> do a child not yet three know? Cept what
> he feel, maybe, what he see. This been
> in yo mind a while, huh? I watch him
> in the rear-view mirror, the thin black
> face, the long-lashed eyes that hardly blink.

> Yes, he say, yes; what that sign say?

> That
> I ain't saved nothin, not for this day.

Some

He was sleep and so missed the Friant lights rowed
    across the night, improbable stars

glimmering above the thick concrete
sides. We parked at a distance from the cars

above the dam and the lake it holds.
The man *takes his hand, helps him*
climb the restraining wall and, once
over it, leads him beyond the rim

of light. I wait in the soft dark,
still tinged with the day's dry
heat, and finally hear the voices,
hear the laughter, see their forms, my

thin black boy, this honey of
a man and the tension along my jaw
will ease. I store this vision against
the day, against the terror of that dawn.

time

I don't always hear him when
he hit the floor in the morn-
ins. Sometime I just feel. And
I turn over and there he
is waitin to climb in my
bed and talk. Wow! do he talk.
Ask me why I wash the bird
crap off the car, tell me he's
gettin bigger and I'm not,
all about his good ideas.
I grunt in answer try to
keep my eyes closed finally
tell him keep quiet it ain't
yet eight o'clock. One mornin
like the rest: he only three.

Mom? This another mornin.
Mom, what my last name? And I
tell, pullin him closer to

23

me. And what yours? I say it,
but he know. Can't our names be
alike, the same? His thin arms
the circle of my own. He
hold me to this world not just
one spot. People don't belong
to you. You belong to them —
but only if they let you.
I tell him we get our own.

later . . .

But it will always be my breath
that catches on the memory
of trying to find the father
to tell him we had made a son
Be my stomach that tenses
keeping back the bitter words
I try not to speak
before my son.

It is my cheeks that are ridged with rage.

Any Woman's Blues

every woman is a victim of the feel blues, too.

Soft lamp shinin
        and me alone in the night.
Soft lamp is shinin
        and me alone in the night.
Can't take no one beside me
        need mo'n jest some man to set me right.

I left many peoples and places
        tryin not to be alone.
Left many a person and places
        I lived my life alone.
I need to get myself together.
        Yes, I need to make myself to home.

What's gone can be a window
        a circle in the eye of the sun.
What's gone can be a window
        a circle, well, in the eye of the sun.
Take the circle from the world, girl,
        you find the light have gone.

These is old blues
        and I sing em like any woman do.
These the old blues
        and I sing em, sing em, sing em. Just like any woman do.
My life ain't done yet.
        Naw. My song ain't through.

c/o Ambush   c/o Mike

The rain-slick summer streets was
never really deserted and I drove
them. I would trip through
neon-lit city nights tryin
to make it fast through all my
young woman years till I could
be old and not be called on
to love no man, but just to
have what I have suffice and
all this wantin be covered by
a spreadin body, buried
in a old woman heart.

        My
mind was takin me through so
many changes and they real-
ly wasn't my mens, was too old
to play at bein my sons.
They was brothers in the way
we want to think they all can
be when a woman need a
man, not just for beddin or
even holdin but to say
in some other way you is
woman to my man.

       So I
was c/o Ambush or of
Mike; I would feel and they would
feel and sometimes speak and all
ways listen, jump into my
case, gimme back me in a
new relation to myself.
They dark devilish faces
would smile or go quiet and

always they eyes, well, they'd be
lovely, fierce but holdin a
young and aged peace. And I
love they young bodies and the clean-
ness of they soul and all that
beauty we guess at cause we
can't ever know the whole but
just sense it in they walk in
they stand in they flashin smiles
they quiet and lovely eyes.

Home

Home, *n. 1.* A house, apartment, or other dwelling serving as the abode of a person or household; residence. *2.* A family or other group dwelling together. *3.* The country, region, city, *etc.* where one lives. *4.* One's birthplace or residence during formative years. *5.* A place natural or dear because of personal relationships or feelings of comfort and security. *6.* A peaceful place; haven.

I resolved to be very careful about who entered my heart. I didn't put up a sign saying, transients and vagrants not allowed—there is a distinction between a wall and a door, between a turnpike and a path. And shared love lives, even when the people move on.

No, I don't know all the hearts I live in. But I do know the people who live in mine. And I want to be on very good terms with all those who live in my home.

Flo Show

work two ways, baby.
We together and I hear
you breathin, the
air raspin over tongue
and teeth and lips
we come together or apart
and it don't matter.
You mine. I made you
in the private night:
Makin work mo ways than one
and I have put it on yo mind.

I'm cool round yo friends
laugh at yo jive, by-side
you with a smile.
But it is on yo mind
you still feel little pointy
breasts and crisp spiky
hair? Is it what you seen in them
other mens' eyes that make
you have to flo show
me with yo hands
claim me, say this is mine?
"mine" work mo ways than one,
baby.

Drivin Wheel
myth story and life

> *I want you to come on, baby,*
> *here's where you get*
> *yo steak, potatoes and tea.*

first story

The darkened bedroom, the double bed,
the whispers of the city night,
against it her voice, husky, speaking
past the one soft light.

> I am   through you   wholly woman. You
> say I am cold   am hard   am vain. And
> I know I am fool and bitch. And black.
> Like my mother before me and my
> sisters around me. We share the same
> legacy   are women to the same
> degree.

And I ain't even touched what's between us.
A sullen, half tearful thought.
Others lay below the surface of her mind,
rushing, gone, finally caught.

> Not circumstance; history
> keeps us apart. I'm black. You black. And
> how have niggas proved they men? Fightin
> and fuckin as many women as
> they can. And even when you can do
> all the things a white man do you may
> leave fightin behind but fuckin stay
> the same.

> For us it's havin babies and how
> well we treats a man and how long we

30

keep him. And how long don't really have
that much to do with how well. I just
can't be woman to yo kinda man.

second song

my man is a fine fine man
the superman of his time
      the black time   big time
in a mild mannered disguise
revealed only as needed:
      the heart steel   heart stone   heart
and its erratic beating.

                  Inner and outer
rine and heart and running.
Running.   Hanging.   Caught by that powerful joint.
But my man can pull his ownself's coat
come at last to see that dick is just that same old rope.

               Yeah.

                 A mild mannered
disguise: laughing country boy astride
      a laughing goat.

    first fable

We do not tell ourselves all the things we
know or admit, except perhaps in dreams,
oblique reminiscence, in sly yearnings, all
the people we feel ourselves to be.

Except
perhaps in dreams   the people we
feel . . .

        Three. A prideful panther who
stalks a white wolf, a goatish rooster who was lured on
by a grey fox and a head, a body
and, lying to one side, a heart.
The head, the heart, the body had always
been apart. The rooster called
them Humpty Dumpty things and urged
the panther to attack. The rooster was accustomed
to command, ruling the panther through
words he had taught the panther to
talk; the words only said what he wanted
the panther to know. He would crow
or blow upon his horn
and the panther would forget
all the questions he had ever known.
And once in a while, just for show,
the rooster would allow the panther
to have his way.
Now, the panther thought it too good
a body to waste, too good a brain to be
forever cut from its source.
                    Let's put them together, man,
he called. You begin with the heart.
                         But the rooster
knew that rebuilt Humpty Dumpty men have a
way of taking worlds apart, have new ways of
putting them together again. He lived in the world
of already was and it was all he ever wanted
to know.
        Not so fast, the rooster cried.

But the panther had already touched the heart
and for the first time he realized

32

that Not So Fast meant Don't Go. He
could feel something new, something
indefinable pumping through him. The rooster's
words failed to sway him. The rooster, angered,
sank his talons into the panther's shoulder.
The panther turned and, instinctively,
went upside the rooster's head.
The rooster absorbed the first blow;
he was smart enough to know it was coming.
But the second was a surprise, beyond
his comprehension. He died with the question
Why   still unspoken.

                            . . . in glancing asides
we are seen, or in oblique reference. And still
left to answer is how we can pull it all together.

       fourth life

They lie up in the darkened bedroom
and listen to the whispers of the city night;
each waits upon the other
to make the final move to the light
or toward the door. They have met
history; it is them. Definitions from the past
— she bitch and fool; he
nigga and therefore jive — seem the last

reality. And, once admitted, mark
the past as them. They are defeated.
She moves to strap on her shoes.

          You said,

                              and he speaks.
voice and hand holding her seated,

33

his head moving into the circle of light.

　　　　　　You said we are more than the
　　　　sum jiveness, the total foolishness.
　　　　You are wholly woman, right? Isn't that
　　　　more than bitch?

　　　　　　　　　What do it matter, huh?

His hand holds her, holds the wary
wearied question. He speaks, slow:

　　　　Matter a helluva lot. We can't
　　　　get together less we stay together.

His lips brush her cheek; she buries

her fingers in his bush. The question will always
be present, so too the doubt it leaves in its wake.
To question and to answer is to confront. To deal.
History is them; it is also theirs to make.

Lines between Seekonk and Fairhaven

               I wasn't raised by no
river, not the sea and the
milk I said I should get was
only an excuse to be
out in the day, to find the
water and not to wait the
ringin phone, the key turnin
in its own self's lock.

                    The river,
of course, couldn't get it,
movin smooth and steely black
tween concrete banks. I left, headed
for the sea. The road . . . highway . . .
stretch. No end before; no end
behind. This close as I will
ever get to runnin way,
pullin up stakes, to gone. What
ahead of me is behind
me. Not the sea, the river —
I can get water out the
tap. I say it in sleep (that
the only way it can get
said. To admit, then, to the
broke vision, to lose   mine   me

                                        I.

     To surrender to what
probably just one mo chick
shit dream: OurUs   We.

                         And this

the closest I ever will
get to runnin. This car on

some highway, halfway tween there
and there. I wait the ringin
phone, the key turnin in its
own self's lock. Jesse comin
home.

Blues is Something to Think About

A traditional statement about
a traditional situation
with a new response,
Or,
another ending for
One-Sided Bed Blues

I say I'm lonesome now,
         but I bet' not be lonesome long
Yeah, I'm lonesome now,
         but I don't need to be lonesome too long:
You know, it take a do-right man
         to make a pretty woman sing a lonesome song.

The Peacock Poems

. . . I never neva thought I'd sing this song . . .

The Peacock Poems: 2

This ain't the beginnin; maybe it's the end

I'm not gon tell you my story; I know what
you'll say: Sister, that's where we all been.

                                             I'm still
is where my child can't hold me; I just slip through
his arms and I know nothin's gon darken my
door. I walk the streets cryin, I bes; I bes:
I don't even know what that means.

                                       I been the
strong sister, the pretty sister, the one with
no mens — Maybe that was a beginnin, the
mens, the no holdin, no touchin, the no one
to lean . . . My back never was bent, just the self
I held in. I don't know what it looked like at
the beginnin only now at the end. And
if that's what I look like I don't want to see.
And that was a beginnin, to look in the
mirror and not want to see what you see. All
this other — the pretty sister, strong sister
the one with no mens — that all come in between.

Yeah, that's all our stories; that's where we all been.

This ain't that beginnin, but — Yeah. It's that end.

The Collateral Adjective

I sing my song in
a cycle a round
spiral up spiral
down the adjective
has little to do
with the noun

          The round
is showy and loud
proud like the noun it
designates person
place thing. To find *place*
call name (and thing is
a greased pole So much
to gain and nothing
to lose: the noun has
all the lines and the
lines, they cover all
the pain.

        Spiral up
spiral down. Cycle
the round circle the
song. Without a drum
that sings soprano
the tongue's only a
wagging member in
the void of the mouth
speechless in the face
of what it has said.
I never never
thought to sing this song.
The adjective the
noun — This is not my
idea of a game.

The Peacock Poems: 1

the trimming of the feathers

I wish I could still stay
down by the fire at the end of the row
and jes watch the baby but Daddy
say I'm a big girl now

not big enough to have my own sack
jes only to help pile the cotton
in the middle of the row fo Mamma to put
in her'n. I gots to keep my jacket button;

it's cold. Mamma say I move
mo faster I wouldn't be feelin it so much.
I can't do what her and Daddy do move
slow and fast togetha and get a bunch

of cotton and keep warm and watch
the baby, Le'm. Maybe I get old
as Jesmarie even Ruise I can do a
hundred pounds a day hold

the baby — but she won't need no holdin
by then. Mamma sing Daddy hum.
He pickin the row side Ruise
and Jesmarie and they pickin side-a us. We come

early fo it's even light and Mamma
face be so dark under them white
head rags and by the end of the day
they be dirty wid sweat. It be gettin on to night

then. Us all be tired. I be thinkin bout
the beans Mamma cook. Jack
come wid the bus. Daddy take
the baby and Mamma drag the sack.

Mamma and Miss Irma talkin. I
like to hear em say, Chile
don' I jes know it!
I like how they shake heads and smile

When they talk they be lookin like
they really do know what each
others mean. They makin fun
and sometimes Miss Irma reach

ova, tap Mamma hand
that's when it's a cold low-ratin
she gon say. Chile. She reach. Niggas
be babblin that love somethin

scandalous, talkin that talk even
when it ain't nothin but hello.
Chile, Mamma say, don't
I know — talkin pretty and slow.

These kids daddy . . . babblin and talkin —
ain't nothin I can refuse him. They laugh
and shake heads; Miss Irma reach:
And I bet they all knows that.

the killing of the birds

I member we went to the hospital that day.
        The only mirror in the house a small
        piece we keep in the kitchen window
        sill. Mamma barely tall

        enough to see in it but she stand in front
        of it puttin on red lipstick, water
        wavin her hair that she usual
        wear in braids. The light catch yo

        reflection so you really can't see
        so good but she stand there anyway
        and when she finish that she oil her legs
        wid vaseline and knot her stockins so they stay.

She put on a flowered dress that make
        her skin look shiny black.
        Miss Irma tease bout how fine
        she look, she say my husband back

        from that TB place; he out to the County
        now. When we get there me and Ruise
        and Le'rn went to play while Mamma
        and Jesmarie stand at the window by the trees

        and talk to Daddy. After while
        Jesmarie come to get us; it be time
        to go. At the window Daddy was screamin
        bout some man and Mamma was cryin.

A Pavonine Truth

I ain't never left this town
    but it's like I been around the world
Ain't never left this one lil town
    but I might as well have been round the world.
Yeah, you know the streets
    can put a hurt on just about any young girl.

Good lovin love
    can put you in a lot of pain.
I know it's funny peoples,
    but good love do cause pain.
Make a woman wonder
    when her man say, let's try it again.

    Some men call me sister,
    some, the queen of the earth,
    the bearer of all life.
    But what really would groove me is my sweet man
    callin me his woman, his wife.

Life put a hurt on you
    only one thing you can do.
When life put the hurt on you
    not but one thing a po chile can do.
I just stand on my hind legs and holla
    just let the sound carry me on through.

    Take yo self to get self togetha
(ain't it funny though that it
    Take a woman to make anotha one pretty
    but take a man to make the beauty shine true.
    Baby, you gots to keep on lovin me:
    My natchal life be dependin on you.

This a Rap on Yo Do'

After you been with some body
Somebody that been diggin on you
It be a long time fo you
Can be with somebody new,
Some body, yes, take a long time to get
     with some body that's new.

You don't be hungry
for jes any ole lips
Naw, not fo somebody new,
Naw not jes fo some body
Some ole lips jes cause they new

I ain't been with no body
Cause I want the one I knew
Naw, I ain't been with nobody new
But still I'm hungry fo a body
Yes, so hungry
But jes only
Hungry fo you.

The Peacock Poems: 3

You know it's really cold
when you wake up hurtin
in the middle of the night
and the only one you know to
call is the operator and she
put you through to the police.

The Collateral Adjective

chorus

Whatever we knew
we forgot sometime
ago trying to
track the noun to tell
the adjective from
it (spiral down)
Our song is larger
than life (which is a
bitch if you live it
but then it don't strike
twice it's the lyric
which is us which is
also life but we've
been carried away
in what's become a
mindless tune. It's as
though the song's more
important than us.

I never never
thought to sing this song
The adjective the
noun the tongue the drum
the spiral the . . . I'm
talkin about more
than just love. But then
I think you knew that.

49

The House of Desire

This is really the story of a
sista who was very too-ga-tha
in everythang but life. You
see she was so too-ga tha
she had nothang but
strife. Everyone thought

because she was so
too-ga-tha she didn't
feel pain and the men she went
with felt just the same. They got
to-gatha with her and then, once they
were, left in most un-togatha ways.

Her end was a black one without pain,
tears of strife. She finally
concluded there's no earthly
use in bein too-ga-tha
if it don't put some
joy in yo
life.

this city-light

Oh, I see myself as I was
then skinny little
piece a woman dying to
get to Frisco and change. I
couldn't see the worn patches on
my coat, only the suede and
once late at night I climbed through
a window into a room.
It was bare the pot up in
smoke and the nigga was gone.

I see myself as I was then
skinny little woman-girl
sitting in a third floor room
a voice floats up from the street
calling me to prayer and once
in answer I went to the
door. There was an old woman
there crying Belle. Belle. Belle I
wet myself and falling up
the stairs.

       (He asked once to tease
what I did *jes fo* fun. You
don't smoke you don't drink you don't
fuck, was the way it was phrased
and the words, no I don't fuck
unless it's with you, never
got said and I passed it all
off as one more hip joke.

                 Oh,
I could say more — there was
the day we crossed the Bridge, we were

perched on the back of the truck.
I never saw the bay quite
like that again: Oakland a
dream city I was leaving
behind; Frisco a city
of dreams I wanted to make
mine — but these three things would still
stay the same. I came to the
city to live on a hill.
I am the bird that was plucked.
I am the woman that was

III

the peacock poem

1

We are
ready for the night
have done the final
chores spoken of the
earlier rap emptied
ashtrays cleared the notes
and records from the
floor. Tiredness pulls
at my legs heavies
my hands as I wash
my face then shrug off
the robe. I bump the
bed in darkness and
fumble at the sheets.

Asleep you reach for me your body
curves around mine. You breathe even and
quiet now and briefly touch my breast my hip. I
believe you know it is my hand you
hold know my neck beneath your
lip.
And I am
satisfied:
You love me.

2

He say
I'm beautiful and
for real chant about
my blackness cause that's

53

another way of
sayin for real for
beautiful for him
and the purple dusk
of every winter
evenin belong just
only to me and
to him. I lay up
beside him and it's
us togetha in our own selves house
in our own selves bed in the dark. the
dark and ahhhhh. it be so good. good to be
beautiful to be real be for him to be
more than one. It's enough. I
know my man lovin
the way
I
struts my stuff.

IV

What is love if it is only
known through words saying it would
be hard for me to leave you?

Some words, seldom spoken
and then whispered only, I
sigh in dreaded visions, smoke
engendered dreams of what might
be or is:

Love, in trying
for good, can jam what it seeks
to free, be *too* instead of
so. And when that trick comes down

54

"I" just isn't big enough to
cover the distance between
"love" and "you."

Postscript

                I offer my
body in the silence of
love-get/love-give to fill in
sexual satisfaction
the space between the words I
have put on this page.

V

the house of desire

The house feels unfinished like
a bird whose feathers have molted or one
that's been stuffed. The wind whistles
under the doors and the toilets run.

There's a voice at the window that calls me
by a name only the brotha should know.
I'd have to leave my house to answer
yet one night I was tempted to go.

The brotha says I got a good
house here. He don't know that night's
temptation, the voice, like a devilish wind
slippin in the window that doesn't bolt right.

The house old as me. They don't make
em like this no more and, like the brotha
say, I got a son. Think
about the sun when the light gatha

in the windows and the floors is all clean,
about you and the house waitin

for your son to come in; your child needs
this house. The brotha is right — comin

on strong like he usually do — but
sometimes I think if he really cared,
then . . . would he leave me so much on my own
to cry and get scared?

The Peacock Poems: 1

A ship
A chain
A distant land

A whip
A pain
A white man's hand

A sack
A stove
A cornhusk bed

Couldn't bend Grea'gra'ma's back
Never lowered Gra'ma's head.

(After an anonymous poem found
tucked in a book
in a library.)

The Finding of a Nest the Coming to a Roost

vanje speak with me

Girl, I could have stood it if he'd just
said we evil and hankty, they say that
so often I take it as their way
of saying love. Naw, the brothas in
this survey said we jive; we don't know
how to act around a man, that all
we want is money, that they tired of
us always having our way, tired of
us leaving grease spots on their jackets
when we put our heads there. Said they want
women that show they black and men, too.

I felt like I'd offered food to some
one I'd been sharing with a long
time. And because some busy body
told him it was poison, he refuse
it, won't even examine it to
see if it's true. I tell him, hey, what
ever you got to share, I don't listen
to what nobody say; I go on
and try it before I say whether
you lied. Can't you do that much for me?
But he go share with someone else cause
he say my food ain't no good. I don't
know whether to crawl or cry but I
do know I don't want to share with no
one else.
        I told the brotha that, but
I could see he thought that was jive, too.

Aw, yeah. I'm a ol woman
now but I still remembers
the days of my youth and they
was somethin — I was too. A
baddd mota scoota but not
no heart-breaka. Naw chile I
could put a broken heart on the
mend set a good man at his
natchal ease jes by winkin
my eye, wavin my hand. Mens
used to would tease me bout my
butt say it took half a
hour to follow me round a
corna. It is long and
I ca'es it so you can set a
tea cup on it and not
spill a drop. Oh, I knowed some
good mens in my time, real mens.
What else you calls it when a
man packs you up and leaves a
good farm cause he don't want no
white mens fumblin unda yo
clothes. Sho, he coulda killed him
and been killed hisself. That's a
ticklish problem and he choosed
the middle way, the one that
kept both his soul and body
live. Yeah, I knowed one to do
that and othas did mo stuff,
did what they had to do to
please a woman like me . . . and
they all talked about my hind
parts. Say when I move and I
still can you know — don't let

59

this ol age fool you now, chile —
they tell me, say, it be like
a leaf shakin on a tree.

. . . and vanje will deal in spades

I'm going out and screw;
call me up the Player. Can
you dig on that? I got to
have arms around me; have a
man's body with me telling
me I'm the only one do
what I do. I want to feel
all that other brotha's words
coming, coming and coming
out of me, coming back on
to them cause girl I know they
can't believe that shit is true.

sista sadie

Aw, yo'alls calls it by some
dif'ent names; back then it were
big daddy little mamma
sweet mamma my main man or
jes only babe. It all come
down to the same thang: love. Love
and takin care. But that don't
mean you be takin low. Aw,
I did it once, maybe twice —
settlin fo what was at
hand steada lookin fo what
might be, should be. What is. But
I seen that that wa'n't me cause
you know, if it's wo-man it's
got to be man that's natchal
that's what god love: a fact. So

60

I didn't take low, not no mo.
I held out fo what I knowed
I had to have. Yeah. I had
me some good mens in my time.
I hold my butt right, I might
get some mo. I even look
forward to the otha side
cause I know when I gets there
it's gon be some sweet man to
say how you doin mamma
I likes the way you walk you
moves yo body like a leaf
shakin slowly in the breeze

The Collateral Adjective

refrain

I am adjective
and noun
            (and this the
first time I sang this
song
        I never heard
the drum sound more than
just that same old blue
note so each time I
heard it   spiral up
I thought it only
one more cruel joke.

I never, neva
thought I'd sing this song . . .

61

The Folding of the Feathers
the Counting of the Birds

I

It's not that the world can ever be contained
in one pair of eyes, the future in one
any body's hands. It should be enough to say
that for right now it is and what come

comes. Every body is a stranger
and if I take this one, make him my own,
what then? We've been lovers for longer than
I care to say, in my mind, in my bones.

If I know that that square chin
was never made to fit in the curve
of my neck, that square body to rest
in my arms, I still don't have the nerve

to let him go. What comes, comes
but I can't make it real, not to move
beneath him in anything but dreams.
Say that I'm caught in the web I wove.

He was the only one to know I
was dying before I was gone
but he wasn't the only one I told.

II

listen to the old ones . . .

The ol folks say if you dream
about the devil you got

to call him by his rightful
name then he won't trouble you
no more. They say that's really
your enemies riding you
and it don't do no good to
cover your head or look for
a protectin root. You got
to call him by name to his
face with your own mouth and know
it, in your dreams. But each time
I try to say his name I
want to say love and I know
that couldn't possibly be true.

III

the tale told by the exorciser

She call me the trickster god
      Well now, you know she don't even not
            even not know the trickster god name.

Yeah, she call me a trickster
      wouldn't believe me when I say
            that ain't my name.

Peoples, the woman looked at me
      Say, what eva name you goes by
            I calls it trickster just the same.

Well now, well now

Well, I got seven inch o' steel
      strapped long side o' my leg
            and, Whoa! this heata know what it is to roll

63

Say, I'm a deep sea diva with a steady stroke
    and afta this iron was cast
        don't you know they broke the mold.

I'm a coffee grinda, rollin pin, a horn
    my stuff long as many mens right arm.
        I'm the one knock the devil down cold.

        So come on to yo deep divin daddy
        Come on here, mamma sweet
        Come to yo strong strokin pappa
        This where you git yo trick and yo treat.

(If they ask you who sanged this numba
* You can mention my name*
* Say, It was The Diva, he been here and gone*
* Tell em, say, It's the TreatMan, the Singa and the Song:*

*   I am the first invoked*
*   no one passes the street*
*   without calling on me*

He is the cross Not the christ
the waters of the deep
the island under the sea is home
and in him is earth and heaven
all earth and life.

He is the crossroads guardian
the last born child
speaker for man and gods.

The hesitation blues
the soprano drum
sound the rhythm
that carries his name.

He is the singer
the song   the road
the power   the new world loa.

Listen to the drum . . .

The old people will tell you that
after each battle, don't care who won,
(and my mamma looked in my face as she said it
a good peace have you talking in tongues.

It's all kinds of battles and what makes
you have strength to fight them is what comes
after the battle is over, that peace
make even a sinner talk in the tongues.

Much as you learn from the old ones
what they know is from their days;
it's some things you have to learn for yourself
and you take that and add it to their ways.

The old peoples talk about
battles and tongues, shrug, say: Life.
But peace isn't always worth the battle.
It can cut through your heart with a knife.

The Peacock Song

They don't like to see you with
yo tail draggin low so I
try to hold mines up high. No
one want to know where you go-
in til after you been and
even though I told em ain't
nobody heard. How a peacock
gon speak: I got no tongue.

                            Here
I come with my pigeon-toed
strut and my head is up for
balance and so they can look
in my eyes. See that sty? that
was from beggin; that callus
come from brushin against all
the some ones I met on my
way to been . . . or is it, am?
I never do know. But I
was trying to make em feel
that I need a little heart
rubbin, soul scrubbin; this is
real. But if I'm a peacock
my feathers's'posed to cover
all hurts and if you want to
stay one then you got to keep
that tail from draggin so mines
is always held up sky high.

The Peacock Poems

. . . the lines converge here . . .

Quartet

I piece together my child
hood for my son and this is
more than reminiscence more
than who said or what happened
or what I have done. I weave
the word ritual where time
and pace are meaning, weave it
best in anger and love: You
don't be*lie*ve fat-meat greasy,
huh? as I wield the belt; grunt
behind his good night kiss, say
yo suga almos mo'n one
mamma can stand; giving him
sounds to link what's gone with what
we renew in our coming.

II

If you have to tell someone
the answer, the question might
as well have been left unsaid.
There's no one answer; old or
new, the form the answer gives
itself can take you home and
even walking with strangers
is like being with people
you've always known.
                              I can
say the word is Thunderbird
even recall the price, tell
of wooden gods and what God
love; that's what my mamma told

me. Her rhythm, her tone — now
mine — were keys to Shine whom I
knew before I was ten, to
the monkey signifying
in the trees but I didn't learn
about them at mamma's knee.

III

I thought — he said — like Lit, I
tease a kid's remark that ought
to crack him up (Yet where would
he have heard it? Who's Lit he
asks and sorry now I said
it, shrug and smile. Oh some
ol rhyme we played when I was
young and call to him to watch
for cars as he starts across
the street. Lit, writ, spit, he chants.
The chant floats back to me,
reminder of what I can
and can't give him: While mammas
can talk that Lit-talk to you —
definitely will do it —
you bet'not even *think* Lit
in front of them. And telling
him just that much would blow it.

IV

In a conference room — this
is from a long time ago —
among white and almost white
professionals I capped with
Lit to end discussion and
a brotha responded with

a grin. We laughed like crazy
and though no one else under
stood the joke they knew that in
our laugh the brotha and I
gather and speak as one tongue.

North County: The Dream Realized

I wish I had known this land
before houses infected
the hills and trail bikes slashed paths
across their sides; before heat
shimmered on miles of concrete
roads (which lead to more roads that
stop just short of somewhere and
the arid air was greyed with
smog. This is the nation-state
finally realized an
epidemic fungus growth
unchecked by either will or
way; I am a powerless
part.

    I booted up one day
walked out across the barren
mesa that fronts along my
place down into a canyon
out of sight of the closest
house to say hello to the
ground squirrels the jack-rabbits
and rattlesnakes switching with
a stick the chaparral I
passed. The plants were the only
life I saw — muted greens dry
browns here and there bursts of loud
purple and lighter blues bril-
liant in the spring light. Once, high
up a jet murmured by and

disappeared; some animal
rustled the undergrowth but
that was the only noise.

III

                              I
went on, not pretending to
be gallant pioneer
conquistador noble red
man or any who claim this
land as theirs by god-given
right. I am as I was
                         The
town-bred descendant of slaves
who like a tumble weed a
seared blade of johnson grass is
moved and stilled as the wind wills.

For Ronald King Our Brother

whom we love, whose actions
are rooted in our common rage
and whose pain we were powerless
to ease, this poem for the present.

It cannot recall the explosion or
quicken the earth bound body
or make any single past present
to be changed or lived again.

Poems are crafted thought, channelled feeling
and now . . . Now. Yes, and living
set in one moment of timeless
time   always and love.   Love.
We hope it is not too late:

                              We rock you
in the cradle of our soul.

1 Poem   2 Voices   A Song

for Sherman McKinney

his body be arched when he play — like Miles —
only leaner   legs stiff
hips forward   and the top
of him   seem like it drift
his shoulders be hunched   protectin his gift

    He put horn to lip and blew
    that he had been through the world
    blew against rock beats in clear
    soprano tones.

he said it be like a battle —
him and that horn — be pain.
I know it like an hour with the blues
blowin help him call his name.

              Now,
    fragmented by the
    tripping lights, the band
    is a fusilade
    a kaleidoscope
    of sound. And then. Then
    he moves, arrogant,
    slouching across the
    stage and his raucous
    voice reverberates
    in the hand-held mike
    rapping, calling out
    a litany of
    heroes: Lummumba.
    Mao.   Martin.   Malcolm.
    Jackson. . . . yeahyeah. Yeah!

he speak when he see a brother
wave   say   what it is, dude?
they nod   say   you got it   man.
he smile cause he know it be true.

this sherman song   the one he blew:

    I been through the world
    (hear it.   hear it.   hear it   feeeeel
    it.   Blow!)

        but only
    the best has touched me.

I Sing This Song for Our Mothers

I'm Odessa Son

I was a man full growed
when the otha folks freedom come, had
a wife and sons o' my own
and wa'n't nary-a-one o' us
eva belongst to no one but us selves.

I tell you now what my ma say, jes
the way she tell it to me.
I want you to tell it to yo woman,
to yo sons; to yo daughters most especial
cause this where our line come from

Sister: *sister   blood   blood   sista*

sound and wind as it roars through fire
the still of the earth as it soaks up
            rain   all

Odessa

They come to get me in the night
the brothas; I tell you how
they name is called. Big
Nathan — he was side-a me on the
chain — Proud Cully what had
the file and Harker what
be the daddy to you now.

Jemina gived them the key
and say she be wid us by'n'by
say to me praise the lawd you
and yo chile be free. I say
Jemina this what in my belly —

79

and that was you — be free wid
me in heaven or hell
but we don't neitha one be no mo
slaves in this here worl'.
Harker say talk make us all slaves
we don't mind out; us got to catch
the path while it still dark.

We two days on the trail. I had
you in the wilderness unda
neath a tree. Nathan and Cully
hold my hand while Harker birth you
and when the pain got so bad I call
the name of the man what
put you here.

        I say yo name
now and that be love. I say
yo daddy name and that be
how I know free. I say Harker
name and that be how I
keep loved and keep free. keep me

Sister: *earth and loom*
    of heaven spring song in the
      passion bird's throat

   sister.   sista.   blood.   all

Mayri

I mean, I really didn't know what was
happenin. They was peoples we'd picked
up at this party — one dude knew some
one Vernon knew and that was enough
to get em a ride. It was obvious
the chick was wasted and the cats wasn't

80

too far behind and I told Vernon
let's just take her on home and he say,
well, you know she really is with them
and the other cats was sayin yeah,
man we still got time.
                                    And, I mean, I
really didn't know. I just want to get
this chick home; wanted my own ass out
that car. I just met this dude my own
self — thinkin bout Vernon, you know — met
him the other week and you know
I ain't never liked no drunk peoples
no way; they either get sick or want
to fight else start cryin and I just
can't be dealin with em no how. But
the chick at least'd had sense enough to
sit in the front with us and finally
I just told Vernon I wa'n't goin
a notha fu'tha with these drunk ass
dudes and some one say, man you gon let
this broad rule yo mind.
                                    Vernon look up
at the rear mirror look over at
us, say, hey man you know this chick used
to live on my street. What you call her?
Mayri? yeah; she still go round with Walpa
Dee? And he go on like that bout Walpa
Dee, what he do what he did what he
done. And I still ain't hip to what's goin
on, just hopin the chick don't heave in
my lap and tryin to make out what
they was sayin in the back seat.
                                    Well,
they break in on the Walpa Dee stuff,
tell Vernon a street and after he
put em out he tell me just what had

81

almost gone down and I say whaat? kept
sayin why cause trains just somethin you
hear about; they don't get pulled on you
or real peoples, not while you in the
car and Vernon mash in a little
harder on the gas. Ain't no way you
can be in the streets too long without
bein on em and that's all he say.

And it's like you know what you don't wanna
know, you know? and when we get the
chick to her mamma house I just start
blabbin right there in the entry hall,
ma'am I swear ain't nothin happen to
yo daughter I swear she all right and
she a big hankty lookin woman
knowin all the time just what I mean
and she push the chick — young girl, too — on
in the house mumblin bout no good daughters
what mess around with low down scum and
how they all gon come to a bad end
and close the hall door in my face. And
I just stands there in the dark with Vernon
pullin on my arm, I swear ma'am ain't
nobody did nothin to yo daughter
she all right but I was still cryin

> Sister: *a scrawl on*
> *the wind   a growl in*
> *the belly   it wasn't always so*
>
> *sista   sista . . .*
> *who calls on your name . . .*

Ruise

I never thought to see us
grow old, our waists thicken, our
children move so quickly to-
ward being women and men.
I have of course; but to see
the woman of your hands
is not to know the girl
who took the womanme in
saw so clearly what it was
that would save me for my
self and so let me be a
child again.
                    The long waisted
body   the long straight neck will
soon disappear in folds of
aging flesh but not age not
added flesh not even death
could wipe away what the strength
of your love and anger trace
in the still deepening earth
tones of your face.
                    I have no
daughters to be the woman
you are and your own is still
becoming

            aerated loam
and fire   the song some bird will
sing   sum and homage   sista

    sista.   sista.   been and is

Communion in a Small Room

for sherley:
whose epigraph I stole
to make the blues — blue!
          —Michael S. Harper

"I give it to you Michael"

It's not enough to sit here
and feel the soft explosive
wow! the silent yesyes, speak
it mouth the awe full god
damn. (That don't make it real

"I give it to you Michael"

                         My
words but they don't answer your
call.

"I give it to you Michael"

        I am not,
                  your audience.
The line converge here, spread

"I give it to you Michael"

We live in that pattern, are
us, now; are all.

"I give it to you Michael — "

             No. (That ain't
Truth. It has always been ours:
Speech verifies communion
between living and living
quick and dead in this small room.

I see my life . . .

I see my life by my son's
eyes   know his mind is in some
part my own   that he carries
me as he moves through the world.
I am some percent of the
sum of my mother and my
father   of the grandparents
the old ones from whom I get
the shape of my hands   my head
maybe my walk and the eyes
that stare from this face. I don't
know all that comes through them to
me and him who are now their
factors in the world. Yet I
am me; he is he.

II

           We're named
in the sight of the people
in our family houses
in each of our own hearts. I
didn't learn how to call myself
until I was twenty-four.
I cling to the secret child-
hood names only a very
few can know.
           I gave my son
four names; he added two more.
In the privacy of his
own room he calls himself by
others I may never know.

III

My son springs up from the bottom
of the pool   head back   eyes closed
water sheeting his body
with light and caught like stars in
the dark burrs of his hair. It's
not the sun whose shine dances
on the waves. That is his face.
And although I see the name
he has named himself I would
never tell it even if
my mind   my mouth   could say it.